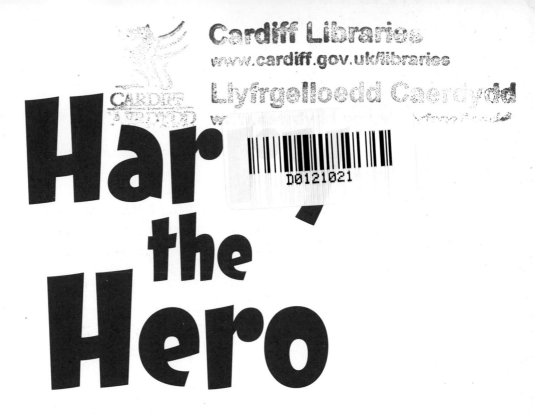

Harry

the

Hero

Written by Tony Bradman

Illustrated by Martin Chatterton

Harry's new school looked great on the website.

Close up, it seemed ... different.

In fact, it looked scary.

I guess it could be worse. It could be ...

... raining. Great.

The playground was a busy place. Harry tried to creep past the boys playing football.

Oi, new kid!
You owe us a ball!

A group of girls saw him sneaking past.

Is that the new boy?
He's so weedy!

And then he bumped into his new teacher.

Ooof!

Harry sat at his desk. He felt gloomy already.

Harry worked hard in class, but everybody else seemed smarter than him.

Harry had always been good at maths, but today it felt as if his brain only had as much power as ... a stale cheese sandwich.

Lunch wasn't much better. Mum had put soppy notes in his lunch box and Jocasta McSweeney read one out loud.

Harry went up to his room. He tried to forget all about school by reading his comics and playing his favourite game.

SUPER DUDE

Outside, a storm was coming closer ...

... and closer.

If only I could be strong, brave and brainier than a stale cheese sandwich ...

FIZZLE!

CRACKLE!!

ZIPP!

9

Jumping jelly babies!! How cool is this? The only thing better would be if I could ...

Could YOU be a superhero?

Take this simple test to find out if you've got what it takes!

1: If your school was attacked by a huge, scary lizard, would you:
a) Fight the monster and defend your friends?
b) Get your mum to complain to the school?
c) Run away screaming and hide in a cupboard?

2: If a cunning baddie was trying to take over the world, would you:
a) Find their secret lair and defeat them in a colossal battle?
b) Focus on getting your homework done while you still had time?
c) Run away screaming and hide under your bed?

3: If an alien spaceship was heading for Earth, would you:
a) Put on your superhero costume, fly into space and smash it to bits?
b) Ask your teacher if you can do an alien project and start taking notes?
c) Run away screaming and hide under your mum's bed?

The answers:

Mostly As: Well done! It sounds like you're a superhero already!

Mostly Bs: Not so good. You should get out more.

Mostly Cs: Oh dear. It sounds like you'll need someone else to save you!

12

Some unusual superheroes ...

Fashion Girl
Is on call 24 hours a day to save people from style disasters!

Mister Twister
Can turn himself into a tornado! (Not great if you're having dinner at the time.)

Captain Average
Everything about him is, well ... average. In fact he's very boring.

Super Mum
Can tell when you're lying, knows what you're thinking and has an answer for everything. (But aren't all mums like that?)

The Incredible Burpo
Has the power to destroy anything with one belch!

Now, back to Harry's story ...

Harry was a hero! Even better, he was a *super*hero!

Having superpowers was so much fun.

Uh-oh, this doesn't look too good.

I can fly like a rocket ... I can't get hurt ... and I'm just so *strong*! This is brilliant!

Don't be silly. That boy is wearing his underpants outside his clothes! Harry doesn't wear his underpants outside his clothes.

Harry went to bed early. He couldn't wait to go to school the next day.

Everyone is in for a big surprise!

But Harry was in for the biggest surprise of all ...

19

The boys seemed to like the way Harry played football – even without his superpowers.

And the girls seemed to think Harry was the funniest boy they'd ever met.

About the authors

Tony Bradman lives in south London, a place of magic and mystery (truly!), and spends most of his days in the fabulous study of his 85-bedroom mansion, carefully crafting his stories. Sometimes he emerges to visit schools and meet children, who are always far more interesting than adults. One day he hopes to grow up himself!

By day, Martin Chatterton writes and illustrates children's books, something he has been doing quite well for thirty long years. But, as darkness falls, mild-mannered 'Mellow' Mart mutates into hardbitten crime writer, Mr Ed Chatterton. Publishers everywhere tremble at the thought of the two ever getting mixed up.